how to talk t~~~~~

separation

by scott c docherty

Sue Atkins, ITV 'This Morning', BBC & Sky Parenting Expert, author of Talking To Children About Divorce

Divorce, separation and relationship break down is extremely challenging for everyone and can be particularly difficult and stressful for children, so I really found Scott's book wonderfully helpful. It is bursting with practical, down to earth advice and I particularly liked all of the super ideas & games to help children of all ages deal with separation anxiety. It is written in a conversational friendly tone free of jargon and is enormously practical, with advice on mediation & the legal process. There are also some great resources and helpful suggestions of books to read to your children. If you are going through a separation or a divorce I highly recommend you pick up a copy of How To Talk To Your Kids About Separation to help you navigate the choppy waters with more confidence.

Anne Dick, founder convenor of CALM Scotland, first family mediator accredited by the Law Society of Scotland

I like the straightforward advice Scott provides in this book, in everyday and kindly language which doesn't try to downplay the challenges triggered by separation but really helps make them seem more manageable. It recognises that everyone faces a different situation and has to find their own appropriate solution, but reassures them they are not alone on the journey.

how to talk to your kids about separation

by scott c docherty
2016

for
mum and dad

contents

foreword one

There's a revolution going on among family law professionals regarding separation and how to deal with it. Scott Docherty's important new book for separating parents perfectly captures the tone of that revolution, placing him at the forefront of its new influential voices.

The old approach, at worst, was lofty, remote and moralising. Now, in Scott's hands, family breakdown becomes a shared human dilemma, worthy of respect, support and empathy. And the children are where they belong – centre-stage. He clearly spells out the danger of children becoming pawns in a parental power struggle, and reminds us throughout that they are not chattels to be squabbled over, but vulnerable youngsters caught in a disturbing transition that their parents really can do so much to help them survive and thrive beyond.

Scott never talks down. A family man himself, he sounds like one – and one who you might wish you could continue this conversation with over a quiet pint at the pub. He wears his years of experience as a family lawyer lightly, always suggesting rather than prescribing or preaching, and constantly encouraging readers to believe in their own capacity. In this, of course, his underlying message is clear: passing intimate family decisions into the hands of an anonymous courtroom judge may be a tempting default, but should be vigorously avoided unless absolutely necessary.

"Soulful" is the word I come up with in trying to sum up this book. An odd word, perhaps, for the writings of a lawyer; or perhaps not, given how clearly Scott's language and approach help relocate divorce and separation in the field of welfare rather than warfare.

I have no doubt this timely and readable book will help many separating parents or their children. It holds out hope not just for a fruitful post-separation dialogue, but also warmly and even humorously shows us the nuts-and-bolts of how to achieve this.

Christopher Mills
Author, "The Complete Guide to Divorced Parenting" (chrismills.uk.com)

foreword two

I have been a practising Solicitor since 1983 and a CALM Family Mediator since 1994. Very early in my legal career, I realised that our adversarial court system was not, in most cases, the best place for parents to resolve issues and make arrangements for their children following a separation. Scott's book highlights the difficulties often encountered and identifies the many important and often crucial aspects of a separation that the court system cannot adequately address.

A court can certainly provide solutions to disputes between parties and can decide on arrangements for residence and contact. However, these arrangements are often, in the absence of agreement between the parties, imposed by the judge and often do not suit the parties or indeed the children themselves. These arrangements are often decided upon after a lengthy and often acrimonious adversarial process which focuses on past problems and difficulties. This process is usually conducted from very negative standpoints with each party looking to paint the other party in a poor light so that his or her ability as a parent is questioned. The feelings of the children, and what really is in their best interests, is often overlooked. Scott's book emphasises the importance of properly addressing the needs and interests of the children, putting them front and centre in the discussions about their future.

When parties separate, communication between them breaks down and trust is lost. What is required most at that particularly crucial time is for the parties to continue to communicate with each other in a constructive and positive manner. This is far from easy to achieve with so many strong emotions at play. However, as Scott outlines, the need for constructive communication is principally for the benefit of the children, not for the parents. The children very often have little or no say in what is happening around them.

At that very point, the parties should be looking to manage their separation with as little acrimony as possible. They need to consider first and foremost the needs of their children, rather than their own needs. Parties have to be aware of the children's need for information and, most importantly, reassurance, at a time when the family unit is breaking up. Scott's book is all about this crucial, but often overlooked area. Parents do find it difficult to talk to their children about the separation, and to explain to them what is to happen in the future. Scott acknowledges and then addresses these difficulties. His book is full of practical, common sense advice. He offers many good tips on how to talk to the children about the separation and how to deal with the many questions that will arise, the children's reactions to the separation and their needs.

Children are very adaptable. However, the extent to which they adapt, and indeed cope with the separation of their parents will, to a large extent, depend on how the parents conduct themselves separately and with each other. Where the conflict level between parents is high, children usually find it more difficult to cope with their parents' separation. They can struggle to adjust to the new life, largely imposed upon them, often without their input and often against their wishes. Scott illustrates these points by reference to some relevant research in his book, but he does so in a way and with language that is clear and easy to understand.

The mind-set that is required to deal positively with a separation and to make good arrangements for the children is difficult to encourage and promote, especially in the context of an adversarial court action. Children are often of a young age when their parents separate. Parties may then have many years ahead of them where they will have to communicate and make arrangements for the children. If they cannot approach their separation with the correct mind-set, then irrespective of the outcome of the Court proceedings, they may have difficulties for many years to come.

Scott includes a chapter on Family Mediation in his book. In mediation, parties are encouraged to develop a new working relationship. They may no longer be partners, but they will always be parents to their children. Scott explains how the Mediation process can encourage and empower the parties to change their mind-set and to consider the longer term view. He outlines how parties can take control of and manage their separation in a more constructive and positive way.

Scott's style is informal and often light hearted and humorous. This is not done to downplay the importance of the subject matter but, instead, to engage and encourage the reader. Scott's book is full of excellent thought-provoking and useful information and many practical suggestions. His tips and advice will remind parties that the most important people in this process, their children, are given full consideration and that their opinions, feelings and worries are properly taken into account and addressed.

Scott's book is an excellent resource. I would warmly recommend it to couples with children trying to cope with a separation. I would also recommend it to those professionals, lawyers, mediators, counsellors and others, who have a part to play in the separation process.

Nicos Scholarios
Solicitor and Family Law Mediator, Paisley

"if you take anything from this book it's that if you're going through a separation, make sure every day your kids know that you love them, no matter their age (if you have teenagers they might shrug it off but don't let that stop you!). and you might come to realise that everything flows from that."

introduction

who am i?

My name is Scott Docherty. I've been practising as a lawyer mainly in family law since 2002. In 2014, however, I was accredited by the Law Society of Scotland as a specialist in family mediation, and since then have been working with separated couples looking to resolve their issues together on their own terms instead of face to face in court. I'm also a parent. That doesn't mean, of course, that I'm an expert in all this!

There'll be plenty of folks who disagree with what I've written in here, but that's ok, I'm really only interested in you – hopefully by reading this book you'll take at least one or two things away that you hadn't thought about before, but even if you don't, the fact that you're even reading this suggests that you're thinking about how your separation is affecting, or will affect, the kids. It suggests that you're on the right track, therefore, that you want to try and make sure your kids won't end up turning out differently than you hoped because of what you might have done or not done.

using the kids as a weapon

One of the issues I come across regularly arises when the parents I meet haven't talked with the kids about the separation. I mean *really* talked. Instead, over the years I've met plenty of parents who have guided their kids through the separation by using them as a weapon against their ex, or by shielding them completely by not telling them what's going on, or even on the flip side by telling the kids absolutely everything and using them almost as a shoulder to cry on.

Given that I've met those parents in my capacity as a lawyer, you might imagine how that type of approach has panned out for them. What flows from that is the basic idea that as parents you can't always make things better for your kids in the midst of your separation, but you can always make them worse.

I've written this little book to help guide you down another path, one that might lead you towards building, rebuilding, and maintaining a more healthy relationship with your kids after the separation. It's you who needs to lead them down that path, to take responsibility, no matter what your ex might do.

where to begin?

It's a tough time, I don't need to tell you. You're dealing with a whole lot of issues yourself, and at the same time watching the kids react in ways you think you can no longer control or wondering how they'll end up once they're squeezed out through the sewer pipe of separation!

But here's the thing: you *can* control it. You *can* keep in check the impact of the separation on the kids. And it all begins as soon as you make the choice to put the kids first, to make them feel like they can always trust you, rely on you.
Think of it like this. Everything going on, all the arguments about living arrangements, finances, communication, who's getting what,

he said she said, all of that stuff that might be clouding your life right now - think of it as like a storm outside. Think about how comfortable it can feel sometimes when you close the window, pull over the curtains, pour a nice cup of something warm and nestle snugly into the duvet as you put out your mind for a while what's raging outside.

When to tell the kids, what and how to tell them, how to speak to them as time goes on, it might seem totally daunting at first. But if you lock out the storm for a bit, focus every day on creating a comfortable environment for the kids to feel safe to express and communicate with you, then it's a good place to start. I don't mean, of course, that you should enter into complete denial about what's going on. Rather, it's about learning how to shield the kids from what they don't need to know, and trying to see the separation from the kids' eyes rather than from your own.

the long and winding road

Guiding your kids through the separation won't involve one conversation. It'll mean thinking carefully about the things I mention in this little book, and dealing with the kids and their other parent (that's right, they may be your ex but they're still and always will be a parent to your kids) consistently as issues arise.

There'll be times when you think you've not been a good parent, that you've let the kids down and that it's too late to deal with that. It'll feel like a constant struggle, a long road to travel, but rest assured that with a little bit of work then it shouldn't be too difficult to stay on track.

all you need is love

What is it with the song titles Docherty?!! I know, sorry about that and all the imagery! But as for love, it's basic but true – the first thing to bear in mind through separation is that your kids need to feel that they're still loved. Yes, there are a whole lot of other things to think about, but if you take anything from this book it's that if you're going through a separation, make sure every day your kids know that you love them, no matter their age (if you have teenagers they might shrug it off but don't let that stop you!). And you might come to realise that everything flows from that.

what are you waiting for?

So take your time with the book. Dip in and out of it as and when you think it's needed. If your kids are older, let them read it or parts of it and you can talk about what they think, what questions they have, and also pick up on some of the more age-oriented books and websites I've listed later on. Even pass it to your ex. I've written the book so that it's pretty informal, not too long-winded, and so that it's focused only on how to guide your kids through the separation with your words and your actions. How you deal with all the other stuff going on, including dealing emotionally with what's going on and handling the financial and co-parenting wrangling getting in the way of moving on, is a whole other book in itself. That said, I've included some information about family mediation later on in the book, as that might help you and your ex focus not only on how to communicate with and guide your kids through the separation, but also begin to control and resolve a little more amicably your ongoing differences.

Bottom line is that this is just a nudge in the right direction to help you through particularly the early days of the separation, and that although I've written it based on my experience, your kids are different and you're probably one of only two people on the planet who know how best to guide them every day. Just take what you need, therefore, adapt it for your own situation, and never *never* think that it's too late or too hard to make a difference for your kids.

mind the language

One final thing before we move on. In this book I use words like "kids", "ex", and other informal language like that. The reason I do this is because that's pretty much how most normal folks talk about such things in real life. I've found that when lawyers and the court system get hold of a separation, you start to see quite artificial language seeping through and getting in the way. Words like "child". I mean, I've not met many parents who, when talking about their kid in the midst of a separation dispute, have referred to that kid as "my child", "I just want my child to be happy". They'll refer to their kid by name, or call them their kid, or "my son", "my wee girl".

Words like "contact", "residence", "custody", "access" and the like, are all words that parents could do without. In my experience, they lead to a disconnect between parent and lawyer, parent and judge.

They lead to labels being given to the kids and the situations they're faced with, making it difficult to see past positions taken in conflict rather than the interests that lie beneath those positions. Most alarmingly, they can also lead to your kids learning words like that, and I talk about this a little later on in the book.

So for me, use of language in a separation is very important, and I've found that by being as natural as possible about that, by speaking with parents in every-day language rather than the impersonal, lawyerly nonsense you might have come across already, there's a better chance that you'll be at ease with it.

That said, I do admit that I couldn't use here *all* the natural language I've come across in separations. I reckon if I did so, my book would end up being tagged with a parental guidance rating and put on the top shelf out of reach!

As for you and the language that you might use from here on in, no matter what you think about your ex as a person or as a parent, how you refer to him or her will play a vitally important role in your search for a way to resolve things between you as parents. It can have a bearing on your commitment to the idea that no matter what has happened in the past, this person with whom you no longer have a loving or sexual relationship is still the other parent to your kids. So if you refer to this person as "my ex", "my former husband / wife", "the devil" (!), and so on, it can help settle and solidify in your mind that this person is in the past, that they have no place in your present. However, if this person is a parent to your kids, and if (as I suspect you are) you want to sort things out after the separation and make sure things are ok for your kids, then whether you like it or not this person will continue to remain in their lives. For their sake, if you want to reframe your relationship with this person into a working parental relationship, have a think about how helpful it would be to tag him or her with a label connoting something that's finished, something that's negative – even if you or your ex don't want that new type of working relationship, as I say your kids will still have him or her as a parent anyway, and in every moment will breathe in and digest your words and approach. So for me, your own use of language in the separation is pretty powerful, and it all starts with how you refer to your ex:

How about "co-parent"?

"underneath most kids' bonnets there's an innate need to want to know how safe they are. they're constantly assessing and re-assessing, on a daily basis, the strength of the walls around them, and if they feel secure, it makes it easier for them to understand, to communicate, to explore."

when to tell the kids

the perfect situation

Your separation will be different from others. There's no hard and fast rule. I could tell you right, sit the kids down before the separation, before one of you heads out the door for the last time. And I could tell you that both parents need to tell the kids together, that you need to talk first about what to tell the kids and only say anything once it's definite that one of you is leaving.

The reason there's no hard and fast rule, of course, is that what I've just described probably only happens in a minute fraction of separations. It's like what you'd hear from a parenting expert in the 1950s, where the starting point is the image of the perfect family sitting down at the kitchen table, homemade bread in the oven, working through in glossed-over fashion the 'five golden rules of separation'!

What you're dealing with right now is the reality. I don't know if you're reading this book before you've separated or after, and I don't know how far down the line you are with everything. You might have started with the grand idea of telling the kids before it all kicked off, but then their other parent started blaming you in front of them and the whole plan got ripped to shreds. Or your kids might have caught you completely unawares and asked "why are you crying?" or "are we still going to Florida?" or "why does daddy not love you?", and your brain's gone into freeze mode.

take a deep breath

Yup, it's a good way to begin. Switch off the tv, put the phone on silent, lock yourself in the toilet for a bit if you think it'll help, but at some point take some time to have a think and assess where you are right now. If you're able to take that time, it's likely you'll realise that you fall inside one of three categories: you're having problems but have yet to separate, or you've decided to separate, or you've separated already. The decision, therefore, about when to speak to the kids about what's going on, will depend probably on which of those categories you fall into.

if you've yet to separate

So you've been having problems in your relationship but neither of you have made (or verbalised) the decision yet to separate. The best thing to do here is to ask yourself what the kids know already. Have they heard you arguing? What age are they, and are they of a maturity to chat about what's been going on? If they've witnessed some of the arguing, that might be a decent place to start the conversation – for example, "So you've heard mum and dad shouting about things...do you want to talk about it? What's going through your mind?". Basically all you're doing here is trying to find out what they've picked up. Even if they shut down and say nothing, it's an opportunity to remind them despite what's been going on, that you're thinking about them, that you still love them, that it's not their fault and they can come to you about anything at any time.

Doing that now, starting the conversation with them, might make it a whole lot easier for the kids if ultimately the decision is made to separate. What you don't want to happen is for them to learn suddenly that their entire world is about to shift upside down, as you can imagine that they'd likely take longer to come to terms with the resulting adjustments in their lives. It's not about prepping them for a possible future separation. It's more about if your relationship's not going well, reassuring the kids that it's not about them, that it's ok for them to ask questions and talk to you about what's going on.

if you've decided to separate

In my experience this decision is usually made first by one of you, but either way at some point it'll come up in an argument or at least in a sit down conversation – the idea that enough's enough, that it's the end of the line. Again, how you deal with all that is for another book, I think, but when it comes to your kids, one of you needs to ask the question about when and how to break the news. Obviously it would be ideal if both of you can tell them together, but if that's not achievable, and even if the other parent isn't interested in agreeing with you a consistent approach in speaking to the kids separately, you'll need to take some time to think it out carefully and tell them soon.

If you both decide to tell the kids, try and pick a moment when lots of things aren't getting in the way, like when the kids are getting ready to head out to activities, and if a time like that isn't immediately identifiable, try to be as opportunistic as possible. In other words, you both agree that whenever the chance arises when everyone's in the same room and no-one's rushing out the door, that's when the talk should happen. OK yes, I get it, given the wild craziness of everyday family life, the thought of finding more than five minutes of quiet time together might sound pretty fanciful, but if you both agree to find or make that time wherever possible, if you agree that breaking the news to the kids will be one of the most important things you need to do before the bags are packed, then I'm sure the time will be found, and the same principles apply even if your soon-to-be-ex isn't interested and you're the one being left to explain what's about to happen.

if one of you is already out the door

It goes without saying that if the horse has already bolted the stables (yes, you might have come up with some other animal!...) and the kids haven't yet been told what's going on, at some point very soon in a quiet moment, they'll need an explanation.

Thereafter, that's when the ongoing conversation with them begins, and I'll talk about that later.

what if it's too late?

OK, so you might be reading this thinking *wait a minute, the kids know already, we're past that point.* Is it too late then to start talking with them responsibly about the separation?

The answer's a resounding NO, in case you hadn't sussed that. Words might have been spoken, the kids might have picked up on some bad-mouthing (I talk about this a little later), and you might be thinking that the damage is already done, that the kids are already being affected by the separation in ways you could've controlled if only you'd read a book like this earlier.

So here's the thing: reading this book won't fix that. It won't reverse anything that's happened in the past, but I can pretty much guarantee that what's happened already for you and the kids would still have been out of control anyway. Despite all this talk of "conscious uncoupling" you might have heard celebrity parents harp on about, no separation will ever be conducted perfectly and without some kind of disruption for the kids, so stop beating yourself up. Again, what you're doing by reading this is showing that you're interested in trying to make life a little easier for the kids going forward. As I said before, it's never too late, and if you can commit from now on to talk with the kids as much from their point of view as possible, then it's a good start.

the general gist

What you'll take from this I hope is that whatever your situation, generally the earlier your kids know what's going on the better, again depending on their level of maturity. Your instinct might be to protect them from it all by keeping schtum, but again in general, kids are more resilient than you might think, and you may well be surprised by how they react.

What I've noticed over the years is that the earlier and the more children know about what's going on, within reason of course, the easier it's been for them to adapt to their new circumstances. To my mind, underneath most kids' bonnets there's an innate need to want to know how safe they are. They're constantly assessing and re-assessing, on a daily basis, the strength of the walls around them, and if they feel secure, it makes it easier for them to understand, to communicate, to explore.

It's how you build and maintain those walls that will be your main challenge in guiding your kids through the separation, and the first brick in the wall (there's me yapping on with the song titles again!) will be set when you sit down with your kids early doors, tell them how much you love them, that everything's going to be ok, and ask them what they're thinking.

"give them time to themselves however they react, as they will need it to reflect on what's going on, to adjust and to work out what's most important for them. it's during this time of reflection that they'll come up with the more searching questions about the future, and start to think about how the separation will affect them."

how to tell the kids

lighting the fuse

You might have been agonising over this. You've decided when is best to tell the kids about the separation, but as for what to say, how to deal with whatever reaction they may have, wow, where to begin? I remember one parent telling me they felt like they were walking into a building with a bomb, and I can understand why it can feel like that. You might feel that you're about to destroy your kids' lives, to tell them that everything they thought they could rely on, take for granted, is about to change.

plan a bit

So if that's the feeling chilling your spine right now, before you walk into that building, before you sit your kids down with or without their other parent, take that deep breath again and mull it over in your head. Have a think about what your kids know already. They might have sensed and picked up more than you realise, particularly if one of their parents has left already. Think and prepare a little for how they might react – a range of difficult responses you might expect could include tears, complete shutdown, anger at you, the run out the room, complete disinterest – and how you would deal with that. Go through some of the questions in this book that might crop up, and although you might not have the answers yet because everything's still up in the air, think about them for a while so that you have at least a comforting general response (for example, "I don't know yet, but we both really love you and we'll work it out").

rocking the boat

I've met with plenty of parents who don't want to tell the kids too much, because they don't want to stoop to the level of the other parent who, they think, constantly poisons the kids' minds against them. Interestingly enough, a lot of the time the other parent will say exactly the same thing! The rationale behind this approach, particularly for the parent who doesn't have the kids living with them, has tended to be that they don't want their kids to get upset with them, that they'd prefer to try and make them happy and enjoy whatever time they do have with them.

As I say, I'm no expert, but if you think after separation your kids will be happy and balanced if you focus only on the fun and games, the cinema tickets, the good clothes, you're just kidding yourself. And while we're on the subject, you're kidding yourself if you think that what's most important to the kids right now is the amount of "contact" or "access" or "custody" you can negotiate or "win" at court. In my experience, your kids want the games, they want the time with you, but *boy* do they want so much more than all that.

They want you to build those walls I was talking about earlier, the walls which make your kids feel safe and secure. So don't worry about rocking the boat. If both parents haven't agreed on how to tell the kids or how to speak to them as time goes on, don't worry about what their other parent will say. Don't worry if your kids get upset when you speak with them, because they'll need to know at some point what's going on, and it's best coming from you in a conversation that also touches on why their world isn't about to end, that it's just turned a little on its axis and that although it might take a while for things to steady up, it *will* steady up.

so how to tell the kids?

Well you've planned a bit, thought for a while about how the conversation might go. The next thing to do is to sit them down. Just like that. I mean, you've seen the movie where the battered and bruised hero faces all the odds, where it looks as though they can't go on, but where they do, they always go on. And the best thing for you to do here once you've planned a little in your head is to get it over with, to push through all the agonising about how they'll react and just do it.

Obviously your situation might be different depending on how each of your kids are likely to react and where they are in their own development, but from all my chats with parents who have been through this, I've found that a good way to start the conversation is to sit the kids down together in a room they're comfortable in. It would be better to avoid their own bedroom or playroom, as that's a place they should be able to retreat to as it's their own special place to relax, so best to go for a common room like the livingroom or kitchen. Again, minimise distractions by switching off the tv and getting them to put away their phones, tablets, consoles, books and so on (despite the looks you'll get in return!). Sit at their eye level, look them in the eyes, and tell them that you'd like to have a chat about some things...
...and then just launch into it!

Seriously though, tell them first only in general about what's changing or about to change, and do so with three rules in mind:

1. DON'T BLAME ANYONE
2. ACKNOWLEDGE YOUR KIDS' FEELINGS BUT KEEP IT FORWARD-FOCUSSED
3. YOUR KIDS JUST WANT & NEED STABILITY

In reacting to the news your kids may try to turn it negative, and it'll seem easier to explain everything from your point of view, but remember that by telling them about the separation, you're not doing this to justify to them why their parents won't be living together – you're doing it reassure them that despite what's about to happen or what's been happening, you'll still be there for them.

what to say

Obviously it will depend on your situation, but at the very least the first thing you should be telling your kids is what to expect in the coming weeks, how much they'll be seeing their other parent or you in the short-term, and that you will be there to help them through it. It's a good idea to let them know any short-term arrangements, including what's going to happen with their activities and hobbies. Much of what you tell the kids about the separation will be totally alien to them. They'll find it hard to understand the types of feelings and experiences you're feeling or trying to relate to them. So especially for younger kids I think it's more important for you to focus less on what you tell them and more on trying to manage what's happening to their daily routine.

In other words, at this stage try and keep the chat focussed on the mechanics of what's to come rather than the "why" and "how" reasons behind the separation. If your kids insist on some explanation about the separation, stick to the basics. Tell them only that you no longer get along and have decided to live apart, that it's difficult to explain but the main thing you want to make clear is that right now they are your prime concern, which should bring you back to talking about what's coming up for them.

If your kids are a little older and mature enough, I think it's also a sensible idea for you *not* to avoid using words like 'separation', 'divorce', 'splitting up'. It's very likely that they won't want to hear what you have to say, and that they'll pounce on any ambiguity if you're not clear about the separation being anything other than temporary. They should understand that you're not getting back together with their other parent, so don't be too concerned about making that clear for them, even if it's pretty hard to see them upset in the short-term, as the sooner they begin their grieving process the better.

If they have questions, as I say try and answer as positively as you can, but make it clear that these are very big things to think about, that you don't have all the answers, but that as time goes on with their help it might get a bit easier. Keep it as simple as you can, and as objective and forward focussed as you can. Don't lie, don't tell secrets they've to keep to themselves, don't ask them to be a messenger between their parents. Don't let them worry about you and forget to be kids. DO make it easy for your kids to trust you.

the aftermath, and as time goes on

Ready yourself for the worst just in case. It would be great, wouldn't it, if you had the chat, you all cuddled and then moved over to that oven to take out the bread. But what's more likely is that you'll get a reaction that'll feel like the rug's being pulled from right under you. If you have more than one child, each of them might react completely differently, one storming from the room and the other screaming "what did you do" over and over again.

The one thing to bear in mind, therefore, is that again, this isn't about just one conversation. The aftermath will involve many chats, so if the first one doesn't go so well, make damn sure your kids know on a regular basis that you're not going anywhere, that you're open for business, and who knows, maybe somewhere down the line they might realise this and come back to you.

So don't give up!

Give them time to themselves however they react, as they will need it to reflect on what's going on, to adjust and to work out what's most important for them. It's during this time of reflection that they'll come up with the more searching questions about the future, and start to think about how the separation will affect them.

Bear in mind that although the separation may be the biggest thing happening in your life, at certain times it won't be for your kids. They may have other worries like exams, bullying, and general childhood concerns being dealt with before and after the news was broken. They might seek answers from people other than yourself, so encourage them that it's ok to speak to their family and friends, and to continue to go about their usual life as much as possible.

And it's important not to take it too personally if the family they choose to speak to is their other parent - DON'T ASK YOUR KIDS TO CHOOSE!

Again, make sure they know that you're there for them, no matter what anyone might suggest to them, and don't react too negatively if your kids try to push boundaries (see more on this later). Listen to what they're saying to you, and try and work your answers around their points of view rather than from your own.

And let them grieve, let them deny, get angry. Don't shut them down when they try and persuade you to reunite with their other parent. Don't tell them they're too young to understand. Let them take sides, let them try and insult you and make you react.

Just let them be, and be there for them if they're ready.

bad-mouthing the other parent

You'll have your own reasons for how the separation came about. Your co-parent will have his or her own reasons. Both of you will want to communicate those feelings to others. It's just the way it is. It makes you feel better, it gets out the justifications and explanations you need others to hear, and once you've imparted what you need to say it helps you cope a little better with the aftermath of the separation.

It's important, therefore, that you do communicate with others, to seek their advice or otherwise just bend their ears. What you mustn't do, however, is to communicate to your kids your reasons for how the separation came about, or your reasons for disagreeing with their other parent about ongoing care arrangements, rules or expectations and so on. That's something which should remain out of bounds. Whether or not you think what you're telling the kids is innocent enough, just don't do it! It's what is called 'bad-mouthing' and just as unhelpful as slagging off your co-parent in front of the kids, because what you're doing there is to tell your kids your side of a story, a side which your co-parent may well disagree with and which by virtue of that disagreement, over time can open up in your kids feelings of inconsistency, confusion, the thought that they need to agree with you *and* their other parent, to keep you both happy lest you stop loving them.

Why is that though? When you're working out how to tell the kids about the separation or what to say to them as time goes on, why shouldn't you bad-mouth the kids' other parent? Why should you keep your side of the story to yourself?

The hugely and internationally respected Gary Direnfeld once talked about what happens for kids when they see their parents bad-mouth each other. His take on it was something like this: kid sees herself as half of mum and half of dad. Whether he means to or not, dad convinces kid that mum is bad. Kid looks inside and thinks, "so which half of *me* is bad?". Kid then sees mum bad-mouth dad. Kid looks inside and thinks, "ok then, maybe *all* of me is bad". Kid begins to lose self-esteem. Kid begins to think, "well if I'm all bad, nothing that I do really matters. If I get into trouble, it doesn't matter. If I do well, it doesn't matter. So who cares?".

It's a common occurrence I've seen time and time again in separations. So you have to ask yourself if that's what you'd like the legacy of your separation to be for your kids as they grow up. Because for me, it's when kids start to internalise what you're telling them with your words and your actions, that's when the problems start. It really should go without saying, but as soon you start to disrespect your kids' relationship with their other parent or to try and impose your way of thinking on their parenting style, no matter how justified you feel in doing so, it might make you feel better for a while but it will have an effect on the kids you might not fully appreciate until you start to see their behaviour change.

So as my gran always used to say, 'haud yer wheesht' before you say something you'll regret!

discipline

I mentioned earlier about your kids wanting to "push boundaries". So what does that mean? Coming back to those walls again, the walls you need to build to make your kids feel secure, I think it's pretty certain that your kids will push at them and test how strong they are. Each child is different. Their age and level of maturity, and how they react to the separation, will all affect how strongly they push and how much you'll need to focus on discipline.

So as they push you might think: I've built these walls to be as stable as they can be in the circumstances. I've built them for my kids. So why would they want to knock them down?

You might even think: if knocking down the walls is what they want, why don't I just let them?

It's absolutely vital that your kids know not only that you'll try your hardest to keep them safe, to encourage them, to inspire them, but also that the separation doesn't mean you'll bend over backwards to please them, to give them what they want just so they won't prefer their other parent. Time and time again I've met with parents in that scenario - their kids are growing out of control for whatever reason, and they feel they can no longer discipline them effectively and bring them back to the way they think they should be, so they relent, the situation gets worse, and the other parent starts pointing fingers. So be as consistent in discipline as you can so that your kids know what to expect, and rather than just shutting them down for their behaviour, explain as calmly as you can why they can't do this or shouldn't do that – positive encouragement can also work wonders; I know it can be easier sometimes just to react to a negative, but try as much as you can to look out for things you can praise your kids for, as this can help them label internally the kind of behaviour that's acceptable.

Fair enough, you might be thinking right now, *OK Docherty, come up and collect your award for the Ideal World Magazine Parent of the Year*! I know that what I'm yapping on about here might sound pretty unrealistic sometimes, but when you're reading a book like this you'll find that 'the ideal' is something that may well not be 100% achievable, but that rather it can certainly be aimed for. As long as you're heading in that direction you'll know you're doing something right.

And remember, much of your kids' behaviour won't necessarily be connected to the separation or your conflict with their other parent. They'll get into fights, fall off monkey bars in the park having ignored your warnings to be careful, try and manipulate you into giving them what they want – it's perfectly normal behaviour which, in a family that's together, would have been dealt with as best you could, sometimes successfully, sometimes not. So why should that change after separation? Don't let them away with behaviour you think your co-parent is at fault for and you might think, therefore, to some extent is excusable – deal with it in the reasoned way you always have, and only reassess that approach if you feel the behaviour's getting totally out of hand and think some professional help might be needed. Which brings me onto...

getting help

Does it all sound too much? In the lead up to and after separation, lean on your family, your friends, close work colleagues, your doctor, counsellor. Ask them for advice but let them know if they get too negative. When it comes to working out how to speak to your kids about the separation, all you need from these people is positive encouragement – you want to look forward, and you've had enough negativity in your lives, as have your kids up to this point, that piling on more wouldn't do anyone any good.

Getting help isn't just about you though. If your kids are reacting in ways that you can't control or don't really understand, make sure you take advantage of any external help available. It's normal for your kids to show outward signs of not coping well with the separation, including getting mildly depressed, angry and anxious, but when that develops into something more serious like sleep deprivation, continual trouble at school, drug-taking, self-harm, violence and withdrawal from loved ones or activities previously enjoyed, then make sure again that you lean on professional expertise wherever you can. Doctors, teachers, therapists, counsellors, youth agencies and so on are there to help your kids in exactly this type of situation, so don't worry about the thought of being judged by approaching them.

Don't feel guilty about doing so. Reaching out like this isn't a reflection of your being a bad parent. In fact, the very recognition that you'd like some help reflects just how responsible your parental thinking is. I think it's pretty vital that you have to be careful not to mask too much what's going on underneath. When you're genuinely worried or sad about how things are going and you can't see a way out of it all, I'm not sure grinning like an idiot every time your kids are near will convince them that all is hunky dory – instead, it might put across to your kids that despite what you might say to them, actually it's *not* ok to be worried or sad. They might be feeling like that inside right now, but when they look into your eyes and see only happiness and positivity staring back at them, however lacking in authenticity that may be, there's a greater chance they won't feel any empathy from you and end up closing you out.

So if you feel like you're just not coping with things, just remember that you're not in this alone.

"once you've asked a reflective question and you get a response, don't think that you have to come up immediately with a solution to whatever issue your kids are telling you about – it's usually best to listen carefully to the response and follow it up with an acknowledgement and perhaps more questions to explore in more depth what they're thinking."

common questions

what questions will my kids ask?

Obviously I can't include every question that might crop up when you start talking to your kids about separation, as otherwise you'd end up hunting me down to tell your fortune before a crystal ball!

The questions I've included, therefore, are just to give you some food for thought as you go through the process. You'll see that I have listed some questions here, but rather like the stereotypical politician, have left out the answers! In short, the reason for this is that the answers will be unique to you and your situation. So take some time to read through the questions. Have a good think about how you might respond if your kids were to ask you one of them. As I've said before, your answer at the moment might be something along the lines of "that's a really good question; I'm not sure about that yet but it's something we can work on", but if you start thinking now in advance of the kind of things you might say, it'll help you find some strength to be able to reassure your kids a little more.

It's also a great idea, I think, to assure your kids that any questions they ask are perfectly normal, to answer only the questions that are asked by your kids rather than ones you think they might *want* to ask, and to think about an age-appropriate answer in advance (in other words, the younger the kid the less detail needed in response).

the art of imagination

There are quite a few questions here and some might not even come up, but the best way to think about them is not to rattle down the list, rather you're probably better taking it one question at a time, closing the book for a bit and taking some time to imagine your kids asking that before moving onto the next one.

As for imagining, it's a great way to prepare for a conversation. In my very early nerve-jangling days in court, back in the office before an appearance in front of the judge I'd close my eyes, imagine myself standing in court, trying to picture the courtroom and the people sitting there, and then I'd think about what I had to say, the possible questions that might fly my way from the judge. I'd imagine myself being hit with a question I hadn't thought about, but picture in my mind how in that situation I'd take a deep breath, smile, and come back with a response. Preparation was key in this. Nine times out of ten my submissions to the court would never go the way I'd imagined it, but *every single time* that practice of imagining the situation in advance, of planning in general how I'd approach the case, led to me being better equipped to handle the case more calmly and professionally regardless what happened. So what I'm saying here is that the very same art of imagination there can apply when you're planning on talking to your kids.

You've decided when you're going to speak to them about the separation. You've thought about the 'how' part of it I've mentioned earlier. Now just imagine yourself in the room. Picture in your head some of the possible reactions in your kids' faces. Think of them asking some of the questions below, and think of yourself taking a deep breath, smiling, and responding calmly with your answer. This kind of preparation, imagining calmly in advance what might happen each and every time you talk to your kids about the separation, it might sound like I'm advocating some kind of wacky meditation technique, but from my own experience I can tell you that it works, as it prepares your mind a little better for what's to come because you'll have imagined in advance the kind of emotions that, otherwise, might have knocked you for six if you were to face them unprepared.

delaying and repeating

When your kids ask an important question at an inconvenient time, and they *will* do this, make sure at the very least you acknowledge it, and tell them that you'll talk to them later about it. Also make sure that you *do* talk to them about it later. Doing this is also a good technique for when you feel that you've been put on the spot – as long as you always follow up on your promise to talk about their questions later, delaying your answer like this can give you some time to collect your thoughts. Sneaky I know, but it can work!

One other tip here: where you're struggling to find answers to these types of questions, a great way I've found to do that is by answering a question with a question, you know like "hmm, well let's see, what do *you* think?", so I've included below some real chestnuts for you to think about and use if the need arises.

Finally, don't worry if you feel you're being asked a question that you've answered already. Be as patient as you can with them. Your kids won't be processing everything in the same way you do, so they'll understand things one minute but when they go away and think about it, they might come back and ask the same question again to help get their head round it.

Right Docherty, get on with it!

questions you might face

So here are a few that you might face, and remember to think about these one at a time:

Do you still love [me / mum / dad / brother / sister]? (in other words, you might be getting asked *if you stopped loving mum / dad, will you stop loving me?)*
Where is [dad / mum]?
Who's going to look after me?
Will I have to leave my room?
Did I do anything wrong?
Where will we live?
What will happen to [pet]?
Can I have a sleepover with [dad / mum / friends]?
Are we still going on holiday? (be careful not to get hopes up if plans haven't been agreed yet)
What will I tell my friends?
Do I have to go to see [mum / dad]?
Is it [in other words the separation] because I [did something]?
Can I still go to [activities, interests]?
Are you sad with me?

Is [your new partner] now my [daddy / mummy]? (don't get too caught up in what your kids call their new step-parent, focus more on the relationship)

Are you still coming to my [activity, sport]?

When is [mum / dad] coming back?

Why did you break us all up?

Will I get a new [mum / dad]?

Why can't I stay with you?

Mummy says I don't need to go to church, why are you making me?

Why do I have to change school, I don't want to?

Whose fault was this? (dangerous question, don't give a straight answer other than something like, "we've had lots of talks and decided it's best for us and for you that we don't live together")

Who decided to break up?

Does this mean I'll be mummy-less?

How will Santa know where to find me? (think carefully of the memories you'd like to create for your kids in one of their happiest times of year)

Where will my [sister / brother / teddys / toys] live?

Why can't dad's girlfriend just live here with us?

Will we still bake cookies with each other?

Why don't you give me as much pocket money as daddy?

Can mummy come to my birthday party?

[Are you / is mum / dad] going to marry [new partner]?

what questions should i ask my kids?

A good conversation with kids following separation can be helped by questions from everyone involved. So although you might face one or two or even a barrage of questions from your kids, if things aren't going so well and you're facing nothing but blank stares, you might want to fire off a few questions yourself rather than just telling them what's going on. So I've listed below some questions you might want to ask them as well to get the chat flowing, including ones not connected to the separation as this might help break things up a little. And as I say, you might want to use these in answer to questions you've been asked by the kids.

One important thing you'll notice about these questions you can ask your kids (other than the direct ones at the end) is that they're mostly open-ended. What that means is that if you ask these questions you're more likely to get a fuller response. A closed question is something like "do you like your mummy's new place?". The answer to that from a kid may well be along the lines of "yes" or "no", with no further explanation offered, so it doesn't really lend itself to getting your kids to open up a little more so that you can work out what they're thinking and how they're dealing with the separation. An open question, on the other hand, will give your kids a greater opportunity to think a bit more about their answer.

So if you'd like something other than tumbleweeds meandering through your conversations, try to ask a combination of these types of questions, again remembering that it doesn't have to be done in one mind-blowing quiz show performance, rather it'll likely be done over a period of time and whenever it feels right to start talking about it (in other words, not while you're at the shops or rushing out the door to take the kids to school). Bear in mind as well that you might be hit with questions when you least expect it, head in the washing machine or waiting for the bus, so as I say, have a think about these response questions in advance just in case the conversation starts out the blue so that you're not as off-guard as you might be otherwise.

When you're directing questions to your kids about the separation, it's absolutely vital that you encourage them to tell the truth, and that you do so by telling them that no matter what they say in response to your questions, it's ok, that they won't get into trouble or judged for what they say. At first they might not totally believe you, but again it's about building up that trust over time with your words and your actions, so that they realise and acknowledge that what you say is true, that they won't get shot down in flames by letting you in on what they're actually feeling.

And talking of acknowledgement and feelings, make sure you, well, *acknowledge your kids' feelings*. You might not be able to fix everything for them right away, but if you acknowledge rather than dismiss their feelings and thoughts when they choose to impart them to you, it can start to build up that trust I've been talking about, making them more likely to share more in the future. This will involve listening, *really* listening to your kids' responses, and by your words and actions showing them that what they think and what they are feeling are the most important things in your life right now. Don't try and 'talk them out' of their feelings or be unnaturally positive, as you might find that sometimes your kids just want to unload onto you everything they've been thinking about and need your ears, a bit of empathy, rather than your words and solutions. Equally, if your kids shut up shop completely, don't force the issue and only talk to them about the separation when it's clear they're open to it.

Open Questions

These can help you explore your kids' needs, and lead to a better understanding about what's going on, which in turn makes it a little easier for you to comfort them. Open questions can include more specific reflection and hypothesising as mentioned below, and generally are based on the old "who", "what", "where", "why" and "how" approach that encourages something more than one-word responses.

Here are a few:

How are you feeling?
What do you love about me?
What do you love about [your mum / dad / brother / sister / new arrangements]?
What were you thinking about before I came in there?
You look a bit [worried / sad]. That must be horrible. I'd really like to hear about it if you feel like telling me.
What do you think you'd like to do with [mum / dad] when you're there? (prompt suggestions if necessary)
How do you feel when you hear mum and dad shouting?
What could I do right now to make you feel ok?
How are you getting on with [a school project or interest you know about]?

[Where / what] would you like to [go / do] next time you see me?
Who [teddy] or what [toys] do you think you'll take with you to my
house? How about...?
Did you see [tv programme, movie, Youtube clip, Vine]? What did
you think?
I get the feeling there's something you want to tell me. Whatever
it is it's ok, you can tell me anything you like. How about we chat
just now and get some ice cream after?
Can you give me an example about [what your kid just said]?

Reflective Questions

These can be used to shift the focus in the conversation, because it encourages your kids to think about what they've just said or done. Obviously your kids' level of self-awareness and therefore their ability to answer these types of questions will depend on their age and stage of development, so again don't worry if, in response, they look at you as would a dog that's just been shown a card trick! When you're asking your kids to reflect on what they've done or said or feel, make sure you don't imply that you know the right answer – what you're doing is to encourage them to reflect in their own way about this, so avoid starting these types of questions with words like "don't you think that...?" or "why didn't you...?". And once you've asked a reflective question and you get a response, don't think that you have to come up immediately with a solution to whatever issue your kids are telling you about – it's usually best to listen carefully to the response and follow it up with an acknowledgement and perhaps some more questions to explore in more depth what they're thinking.

Here are a few:

You say you'd like to stay with me. How do you think your [dad / mum] might feel about that?
You've told me that you don't like how things are changing. Can you give me an example?
When you say you didn't want to speak to your dad, can you tell me what you were thinking?
Mummy said you were annoyed last night – what was making you feel like that?
What did you think when I talked about [new partner, separation, etc.] earlier?
I see you've drawn [something your kid's drawn about family etc]... (then talk about that)
So what do you think is the most important thing in your life just now?
Next time you [get upset, want to talk], what do you think you can do? (talk to you)
What [nice / no so nice] things have happened this year that you think you'll always remember?
What do you think [I am, your dad / mum is] most proud of about you?
Can you tell me what's been [hard / easy] for you recently?
What's the best thing about spending time with [mum / dad]?
Remember the movie Inside Out? What emotions are running amok in your head just now?

How many people do you think really love you? (run through the list, prompt "do you think...does?" if little response)

So what did you like about [separation book just read – see resources section later]?

When you go to bed tonight, what do you think you'll be most grateful for?

What words was it I used that made you feel like that?

Hypothetical Questions

These allow you to explore possible options with your kids including ones you might have been discussing or negotiating with their other parent. They can also open the conversation up to explore what your kids are dreaming or hoping about, so that you can refocus them onto the reality of what's going on.

Here are a few:

What would you say if [dad / mum] asked you to stay over on a Friday night?

If your [mum / dad] was here now, what would you want to say to [her / him]?

If you could travel back in time and give yourself some advice, what would it be?

Right, let's say you had a magic wand...?

How would you feel if [new partner] came to the park with us?

Imagine you're at [dad's / mum's new home], what would you do for fun there? How about...?

If you could change one thing about what's happened this year, what would it be?

If you could describe in one sentence what these changes have been like for you, what would that be?

If you were President of this family, what would you decide to do?

Would you rather have legs as long as your fingers or fingers as long as your legs?

If I gave you a kiss and cuddle every time I saw you, would you be happy?

Would you rather have all the toys in the world or know that mummy and daddy love you?

If you could be anything at all, what would you want to be when you grow up?

Direct or Closed Questions

These can be used sometimes to manage your kids' emotions if they appear to be getting out of control a little, for example by distracting them with a question about something else entirely. The short answer you'll probably get from direct questions will lead more easily back into an open-type question.

Here are a few:

That makes me think about [something funny that happened in the past]. That was funny wasn't it?

You still trust me don't you? [leads to something like, 'what do you think trust means?']

You still love your [mum / dad] don't you? [leads to, for example, 'and we love you, what do you think that means?']

You know we both want you to be happy don't you? [leads to 'and what things make you happy?]

OK yes or no...?

You're going to be ok with this, right?

You'd tell me if you weren't ok with this, right?

Can you tell me how you're feeling in one word? (then ask what makes them feel like that)

Would you like it if we talked later instead of just now?

Do you understand what's going on? (if not, ask what your kid doesn't understand)

So there are some questions for you that you might face or might ask during your ongoing conversations with your kids. As I've said before though, your situation is unique, so don't worry if you're hit with a question that's not shown here, or if you want to know something from your kids that's not been included in the list I've trotted out. Bottom line is that you should keep open that line of communication with your kids before and after the separation, so that any questions that need answered can be discussed naturally. Your kids may appear disinterested in talking about the separation sometimes, so again don't throw the dummy out the pram if the chat tails off into something they're more interested in, because a good conversation with your kids about separation will need to be moved forward at a pace they're comfortable with, so don't feel you need to tell them everything all at the same time.

"over half the children who lived in two homes because of separated parents were positive about their "divided" lives, and those who had an active role in decisions about these arrangements and were able to talk to their parents about their problems, were more likely to have positive feelings about moving between households."

you are not alone

song titles again?

Yup, Michael Jackson certainly wrote a few tunes! So anywho, in this section I'll be referring to three studies about children and separation carried out around the world, based on three big questions you might be trying to sort out with your co-parent, three questions that your kids may well be mulling over in their heads right now:

one. *where will we live now that our parents are separating?*
two. *if our parents don't love each other, do they still love us?*
three. *how are things going to change for us?*

First off, the reason I'm referring to research studies isn't to bore you with statistics, or even just to prove that I've actually put some real thought and research into all this! The reason I'm doing it is to show you that you're not alone. It might feel that way sometimes, but if these studies show anything at all, it's that what you're going through right now has been gone through before, and will continue to be gone through again and again the world over. That of itself might not make you feel better, but hopefully by looking at these studies you'll pick up a few tips, a few things to think about in speaking to your kids about the separation.

I'd encourage you to read more studies than these on the types of issues that can arise for kids in separation, but the second thing I should say about studies, of course, is that they're not the be all and end all. I've cherry-picked these three because I think they're quite relevant to what I'm talking about. Their conclusions, however, are based only the folks they interviewed and may differ from the many other studies carried out before and after, and although those folks may have come from various cross-sections of society, they're not you. So take from them what you will, but *do* read them as you may well see a few patterns reflected in your own situation.

one. where will i live?

In a study out in April 2015 led by Malin Bergström at the Centre for Health Equality Studies (CHESS), Stockholm University / Karolinska Institutet, the big question was whether there's an association between joint physical custody and psychosomatic problems in kids that lead to stress.

The study was felt important as these days across the western world a significant percentage of separated parents share joint custody of their kids, in other words the kids live pretty much equally between the two different homes of their parents, and the concern was that all the travelling and instability of this type of arrangement might lead to stress for the kids. The study asked 147,839 kids, between 12 and 15 years old and from different types of family backgrounds, about difficulties with concentrating, sleeping problems, headaches, stomach aches, feeling tense or sad or dizzy, and what their appetite was like.

As you might have sussed out anyway, the conclusion from the study was that kids living equally with separated parents were more likely to be stressed out than those in a typical nuclear family. What you might not have sussed out though, was that the study also concluded that the kids living equally with separated parents were likely to have *better* psychosomatic health than those living most or all of their time with one of their parents. This pattern was established in relation to outcomes such as satisfaction with life, risk behaviour, school achievement, well-being and mental health. The kids involved in the study did talk about the hassle of living in two homes, but made it clear that close relationships with their parents was more important.

So what does this have to do with the price of bread?

You'll have been thinking at some point, and might even have been talking with your co-parent, about the huge post-separation questions of "where will the kids live" and "how will they share time between us". The general gist of this study, I think, is that living in more than one home isn't going to be ideal for kids, but it appears to be more in their interests for them than living mostly or only with one parent; and more importantly these psychosomatic 'symptoms' of stress and so on can be lessened by the kids getting the opportunity to have a close relationship with both their parents.

Please be clear though that I'm certainly not advocating that this should be the norm. I don't know what your circumstances are, and it has to be said that every situation will turn on its own axis. This study refers to kids in their teens, so looking at the arrangements for younger kids will involve different considerations. The point in my referring to this (boy do I sound defensive!) is really just to provide some food for thought when thinking about this major question.

So, there may well be reasons you don't want the kids living with your co-parent, or spending as much time with your co-parent. Those reasons might centre on your understanding of what he or she was like to you, or how involved your co-parent was in bringing up the kids before and after the separation. Obviously if there are genuinely major issues like domestic abuse and so on, the matter will likely be way more complicated, but what this study tells us is that over and above how much you might not want or trust their other parent to look after the kids, there's a big question to ask here:

Given the possible resulting stress to the kids in how we design the post-separation living arrangements, should we involve them in the discussion?

I won't lie, it *is* a big question, and as I say, one where the answer will depend entirely on your own circumstances and whether you feel your kids are genuinely old and mature enough to think in a reasoned fashion about it. When you're thinking about whether to involve them, and how to involve them, I don't mean of course that you should consider letting them make the final decision. You need to be clear in your own mind, and also with your kids, that ultimately the construction of post-separation living arrangements is your responsibility. What I've seen help sometimes, though, is an approach where the parents are saying to the kids something like "we're going to decide how you can spend as much time as possible with us both; we've got a few ideas about that but what do you think?". Yes that's pretty basic I know, and you might think that asking your kids this would just end up opening a whole can of worms. As I say, having started to speak to your kids about the separation you'll begin to get an idea about how they're thinking, and whether asking them about shared parenting will end up not helping the situation, so tread carefully, as you don't want to stress them out by giving across the impression that you *are* making them decide (avoid at all costs the "what do you want" approach!) – it's more about sussing out from them any feedback on what's proposed about how they might divide their time between their parents.

Of course, you might find yourself talking to the kids about all this whilst your fingers are crossed behind your back, hoping as you might for the response that they only want to live with you. But all I'd suggest is that when you're speaking with your kids you bear in mind the conclusions in this study. So if you do decide to ask them about how they see things going, and they do tell you that they don't want to spend any or much of their time with their other parent, just have a think about how you might respond to that – you might hate your co-parent's guts and feel the kids would be led astray or neglected, but try to be as objective as you can and suss out from them whether, for example, they're just telling you what they think you want to hear, particularly if you've not been careful with your demeanour and are firing off signals as to what they think the 'correct' answers might be. To you it might feel obvious that they're better where they are, where they've been brought up, where their friends and interests are, and they might tell you or imply that they want to hold onto that, but having looked at this study, you might come to think that more important than all that material stuff is their innate need to have a healthy relationship with their other parent.

Of course, if their other parent chooses not to take up that opportunity, that's another story, but don't forget the idea here that despite what arrangements you might think are best for your kids, listening to them carefully will help you work out what it is about the current or proposed arrangements that might be playing on their minds.

two. do you still love me?

The Joseph Rowntree Foundation has produced a whole swathe of helpful papers on a myriad of topics, and in July 2002 published one on how primary school children cope with family change.

The figures will likely have changed since then, but in 2002 it found that over 70% of kids experiencing separation were under the age of 10 years old. Given that most of the studies back then focused on kids older than this, the JRF wanted to redress the issue. It interviewed 281 children aged 5-9 years old, from four different primary schools in very different catchment areas, about their feelings about family change. Although that's not a huge number of kids, again it's a representative sample you can take from what you will.

The study concluded that parental separation isn't the only source of insecurity and unhappiness for young children, and the quality of relationships they have with important adults and siblings in their lives can be more important than biological kinship alone. The most important thing for kids was how much their parents remained emotionally and practically committed to them after separation. They dealt with their emotional difficulties by playing, sleeping, being angry and showing distress, all coping strategies they were aware about and sometimes even learned in school. For children who needed support, the main element in their decision about who to turn to was trust, something that could take time to establish. Many kids were reluctant to talk to school friends or teachers as they didn't think the school was a safe place, and sometimes they experienced taunts and playground bullying if other kids heard about their problems. Finally, the study suggested that younger kids don't necessarily want more opportunities to talk, and it may be more important for them to 'do' rather than 'talk' (for example, by playing games or learning practical skills).

So what can you take from this?

In talking to your kids about the separation, make sure they know they can trust you, confide in you, rely on you. Make sure they know you're very much interested in helping them through any other issues they're facing that may have nothing to do with the separation, in other words, by not making them feel as though everything is about you and what you're going through. Use some of the techniques I've laid out in this little book and think carefully and consistently about protecting your kids from the impact of the separation, and encouraging them as much as possible just to be kids rather than have them worrying about you (so find other folks to get things off your chest to).

If you get the impression that your kids don't fancy talking about things, don't force the issue, but try and get them involved at some point in doing things with you to help them feel that trust, that bond which tells them without words that you're still there for them. A good technique I've seen used for encouraging particularly younger kids is to draw with them things like family maps you can then talk about, like "can you draw me a picture about who loves you?", or to play certain games with them like those I mention later.

The big thing here is being present in their lives, being a constant in their lives. If your kids are as young as this it's less important to talk with them about the separation, and way more vital that you're simply there for them, that you encourage them, make them feel safe and happy.

three. what's going to change?

The JRF also conducted a study in 2001 of 467 kids aged from 5 to 16 years old from diverse family backgrounds, basically to examine the perspectives of children about their changing families.
It found that a quarter of the kids whose parents had separated hadn't been told anything about the separation when it happened, and that most kids were confused and distressed about it all with only 5% of them saying they had been given a full explanation by their parents and a chance to ask questions. The kids who felt that they had poor relationships with their parents, and that they had been more involved in their parents' conflict, tended to show more adjustment problems.

More interestingly, over half the children who lived in two homes because of separated parents were positive about their "divided" lives, and those who had an active role in decisions about these arrangements and were able to talk to their parents about their problems, were more likely to have positive feelings about moving between households. I don't think I need to elaborate on that, suffice to say that when you're thinking about how to talk to your kids about the separation, remember again that there's a difference between involving them in decision-making about arrangements and involving them in the conflict you may still have with their other parent.

In November 2015 during its annual Dispute Resolution Week, Resolution published the results of a poll which suggested that 47% of kids don't know what's going on during their parents' separation or divorce, and that around 30% of kids wished their parents hadn't been horrible about each other in their presence and tried instead to understand what it felt like being in the middle of everything. It also suggested that half of the kids polled thought that their parents should put their kids' needs first in the separation process.

It may be, therefore, that your kids are concerned less with the fact of the separation and more concerned with the uncertainty of what's to come. Your kids don't need to know *why* their parents have separated, but do need information about where they'll be living, what school they'll be attending, and when they'll be seeing each of their parents in the short-term. Arrangements might change after you've told the kids this, but what you've done already by that point is to open up a line of communication with them, a new pattern of involving them in what's happening that will give them a degree of ownership of the arrangements, a sense of empowerment where it's appropriate, and which could make it a little easier in the future to discuss proposed adjustments.

end of the paint drying

So there are just a few little studies for you. In telling you about them, I don't mean to bamboozle you into thinking that there's only one true way of talking to your kids about separation, and that if you don't follow the conclusions in the studies then your kids will end up looking forward to nothing but a life of crime and punishment!

As I said before, what I hope you've taken from them is that the anxieties you're feeling right now about how to guide your kids safely through this new family situation, first of all are anxieties felt by others all around the world for many years before now, and secondly are anxieties that have been *resolved* time and time again by parents simply trying their best to put their kids first.

Again, you'll feel that you've made some mistakes. The important thing is not to get too hung up on that, and to focus on making sure your kids know you'll always be there for them. If you're struggling with it all, don't hesitate to reach out, as there are many services available to help you.

"applying techniques striking at the heart of your kids' separation anxieties, there will be a better chance for you to have a smooth handover to their other parent or caregiver and for your kids not to be too anxious about being away from you."

dealing with or avoiding separation anxiety

object permanence

OK so I'll admit it now (if you haven't sussed it anyway by reading all this!) - I'm a bit of an armchair psychologist. Much of what follows in this section has been learned either in the pretty fascinating psychology module I completed at university as part of my law degree, or otherwise just as a parent over time and by reading studies and research papers. Don't worry though, I won't bore you with everything I've read about attachment theory and stages of development in children, rather I'll focus more here on the practical things I've seen work in real life with kids of separated parents, things that you might try yourself to help your kids through some really difficult times.

One thing I remember from that psychology module I completed (and I apologise in advance for this one tit-bit of textbook phraseology) was something called 'object permanence', the concept that things continue to exist even though they can't be seen. In philosophical terms: if a tree falls in the forest and no-one sees it, does it make a sound?...

...With separation particularly where your kids are babies or infants, even though they can't see you when you're away from them, if you do things right then in time they'll learn that you still exist and haven't disappeared forever. Once that's learned, your kids might come to realise then that although they can't see you and that you do still exist, this means that you're actually somewhere else *without them*. If left unaddressed, this type of thinking can lead to separation anxiety, so helping reinforce object permanence through games and the little techniques that I've listed here can help your kids adjust and learn that, in time, you will *always* come back to them. I mentioned before about younger kids needing more than words to help them through the separation, so give some of these a try if you haven't already. I've not provided here an exhaustive list of techniques and games you can use, so if you think they're not suitable for your kids, just take from them the basic premise underlying them and apply it to your own games or practices.

Of course, I should say that using these games and techniques should be a must anyway for your kids, and not simply things to do where it's clear your kids are showing signs of anxiety. And if your kids are a little older, although some of the techniques may be designed for youngins the same principles will still apply, albeit you can adapt them to be more age-appropriate.

Finally, as always these techniques are more likely to work well where they've been discussed and applied consistently with your co-parent. I appreciate that may not be possible, but if your kids are showing signs of anxiety particularly at times of 'handover', then make sure at least to try and start a conversation with your co-parent about how you might address the situation together.

peek-a-boo

Yup, try this with your teenager and see how they react! I jest, of course. This is a superb game for kids very early on in their development. They'll look at your face, and when you cover your face with your hands or a cloth, they'll think you've just disappeared into thin air! The magical reveal that follows, however, with its "boo" said with a glowing smile, begins to teach your kids that in fact, you didn't cease to exist after all and that you came back. Doing this repetitively is a pre-cursor for the techniques below, as the same premise of disappearance and return is reinforced in each one of them.

An alternative version of this game is 'where's the baby?', where you can place a cloth or something soft over your baby's face, and again reveal you to them by lifting it off.

hide and seek

This is a real gem of a game for anxious kids. Where your kids are younger or are showing signs of separation anxiety (for example clinging to you, being upset in the lead up to and at handover with their other parent, and so on), then start off lightly. Try doing it in the same room or place, and being silly enough to hide behind obstacles that don't hide you at all, like a thin tree or small chair. This can develop out to going out of the room but making sure you make silly noises so that your kids can still hear you and know the general vicinity you're hiding in. Then the next step will be not making those noises, hiding further way, and so on and so forth.

You can also practice the technique behind this game by simply walking out the room whilst in conversation with your kids, continuing the chat while you're out the room and then returning. This can develop into telling your kids that you need to go into another room but that you'll be back in a minute. Gradually you can increase the length of time between leaving and returning, the idea of your definite return being reinforced each time. In this type of situation, don't leave the room without telling your kids first – give them a kiss, tell them that you love them, that you'll be back soon, and only then leave. If your kids start to cry while you're out the room, you'll have to be strong enough to resist the temptation to walk back in until you feel it's right, as otherwise they'll begin to think that they can control your return.

where's bunny?

The same concepts behind hide and seek can be applied with your kids' favourite toys and teddies. Hiding them and hunting them down together is a great way to extend out the idea of not only you going away and coming back, but also of things your kids are used to and comfortable with disappearing and being found again. You can start by showing your kids where you've hidden the toy and then playing a silly game of hunting round the room to find it again, pretending that you can't see it until they shout at you "it's there, it's there!", and then developing it out from there. For kids, the very idea of leaving their favourite toy somewhere and knowing that when they come back it will still be there, can help reduce their anxiety about things like overnight living arrangements with their other parent.

pretending

Right, shake off for a while all that boring adulthood running through your veins, and cast your mind back to what it was like as a kid playing make-believe! You can go into as much detail as you want, putting on costumes or setting up a mini stage play, but however you do it, a magical way of working on your kids' separation anxieties can be by pretending that you're leaving. All you need to do here is to act out situations where you're leaving the room (or castle, spaceship, dinosaur compound, princess palace...), or where a favourite toy is leaving, but then you or the toy comes back (to rescue the Disney character from the dragon, or to tell your kids about the amazing adventure you've just been on...). Or put your kids in charge of setting up the play and then they leave you or the toy alone before coming back. It gets your kids' imaginations working but at the same time works on their feeling of being safe on their own in the knowledge that you'll return or will be there when they come back.

the magic item

Give your kids a bracelet, toy or item to hold onto when you're away from them to remind them of you, and ask them to look after it until they see you again. It can be something you've made together or you've bought for them, anything really. For younger kids you could create a story around it, like the secret magical amulet that whenever it's tapped twice by your kids will form magically an image of them in your mind so that they'll know right then you'll be thinking of them. For older kids it could be something as mushy as one of those heart keyrings I've seen that split into two for each of you to keep, or as 'non-dorky' as your lucky coin. Whatever you choose, it'll be something that your kids can look at or know they have in their possession when they can't see you, so that despite your physical separation you'll still be present in their lives.

secret handshake

Here's a good one. Make up a silly handshake only you and your kids know about, one that you can use when you're saying hello as well as goodbye. A twiddling of the fingers combined with a pull of the ear and a wink. Or something involving a knuckle-bump and hop, maybe. In an ideal situation you could make it the handshake your kids give both you *and* their other parent, one that's a secret only to you guys, as this could help smoothen the transition a little, but if that's not possible then at least your kids will have something fun that reconnects them with you after a period of separation and to look forward to while you're away.

hidden surprise

Don't do this all the time, as otherwise it'd be expected and lead to disappointment if you forgot. Sometimes you could leave a little message, or a note or drawing in your kids' bag. Just something to remind them when they're away from you that you'll be thinking about them. It doesn't have to say that directly of course, and could simply be something funny to make them laugh. Or if you've agreed with their other parent a trip or activity coming up soon, you could always put in an item that's associated with it (like a toy lion if it's a trip to the safari park, for example) and a message to 'ask your mummy about this'. Again, just use your imagination and if you see your co-parent doing the same in return for your kids by leaving a message, try to encourage and be positive about it.

'who loves me' book

Creating with your kids a basic book containing photos of family and friends is a brilliant way of reaffirming for them the people involved in your kids' lives. It reminds them of important people they can't see at the moment. Flicking through the book with your kids helps them in a number of ways, but in a separation in particular where they'll be looked after by family or caregivers other than you, it helps your kids understand on a deeper level that you're all in it together for them and that you all love them. You can get them to draw pictures of their loved ones next to each photo or even just write the names of the people there. If you can get a hold of a laminator you can preserve it so that it can be used over and over again – just punch a hole in the corner of each page and loop through some ribbon to hold it all together.

re-connection

Similar to the technique earlier about telling your kids you'll be leaving the room but will come back, for older kids a great idea is to talk with them not only about what you'll be doing and what they'll be doing while they're away from you, but also what you'll do together next time you see them. Doing this will focus for them their reconnection with you, so that they can head off safe in the knowledge of what to look forward to when they see you again.

Another important thing to do to help the re-connection is to be boring sometimes! Eh? Yup, it's a subtle technique I've found useful particularly where your kids are spending less time with one parent than with the other, as I've tended to find that the parent with less time tries to cram in so much fun for the kids that they begin to see their time with that parent as fun-time and, more worryingly, their time with the other parent as dull-time (in other words, when the dreaded homework and housework has to get done!). Pour some gravy over that ice cream for a bit. Where both parents try and mix in with the fun stuff some more ordinary things to do, like going to the supermarket or tidying the house, then you might find your kids will feel a little less that the quality of time with each of their parents is different, and that can help minimise some real disruption.

the in-between

You may well have been organising with your co-parent the living arrangements post-separation. A lot of the time parents will focus only on the physical 'contact period' each parent will have, like dad has Friday to Sunday, and so on, and forget about the 'in-between'. What do I mean by the 'in-between'? It's the times when your kids won't see you. Commonly I've come across parents who argue that their time with the kids is *their* time, and as such, *their* time should not be interrupted. Does that sound familiar? Does it sound right?

Phone calls, video chats, texts, and social media contact, agreed or outlined in principle with your kids' other parent, can prove vital in reducing any separation anxieties in your kids. It's not about interrupting parents' time with the kids – if kids want to speak to their other parent when they're not with them, what really is the problem with that? Within reason, of course, lest their entire time with your co-parent becomes a reality tv show for you to watch on video chat!

careful language

One important thing to remember as I've said earlier is that you should keep your kids informed in advance about any living arrangements. It reduces for them fear of the unknown, and lets them plan their time a little better. Be careful, however, about how you put across what will be happening. When they exhibit some distress at the thought of you leaving or of 'having to go with dad', it's ok to say things like "I wish I could stay with you", but don't add in "but your mum / dad wants you to go" or something similar that suggests you're being forced away from them. At handover, remain calm, civil with whoever's collecting the kids, and again, don't talk about separation stuff in front of the kids.

saying goodbye

You might be reading this thinking something along the lines of *yeah Docherty, I wish you could see my kids at handover, screaming at me not to force them to go.* I'm not saying that all of this will definitely work, but if you try some of it over time and develop as best a routine as you can, then one of these days by the time handover comes around you might find those screams a little more diluted. After putting in all that work, applying techniques striking at the heart of your kids' separation anxieties, there will be a better chance for you to have a smooth handover to their other parent or caregiver and for your kids not to be too anxious about being away from you. At the handover try to smile, laugh, hug and kiss, and find a balance between not prolonging the goodbye and again not sneaking off when the kids are distracted. For you and your kids, doing all this can definitely make saying goodbye a little easier.

if none of this works

One thing to bear in mind is that a degree of anxiety about separation in your kids is perfectly normal. Over time and with plenty of focus on the types of ideas I've mentioned here, I'm pretty sure it can be avoided or overcome. As I've said before, however, if your kids are showing signs that something a little more serious is going on underneath the bonnet, take them to see someone who can help, for example their doctor or counsellor, as some external assistance might be needed to address the anxieties and how they've developed over time.

two hard and fast rules

Turning for a minute to my time as a family court lawyer, I can tell you that I've seen separation anxiety and the attachment theory being used by lawyers in various ways. I've seen the old chestnut 'this child has a closer attachment to his mother so should live with her', and on the flip side, 'it is in this child's interests that her loving attachment with both parents be recognised with equal parental contact'. Or even, 'this child is anxious about being apart from his mother for so long, so should spend less time with his father at the moment'. As I talked about earlier on, a lot of labels are thrown about by lawyers, and I've witnessed first-hand general theories about attachment and separation anxiety being bandied about freely without much thought as to whether those general theories actually applied to the kids being talked about. As a result of this type of approach, I've seen plenty of orders made by courts fixing living arrangements for kids with no real investigation or understanding of the immediate or latent psychological impact on the specific kids being argued about.

So what does all this mean for you?

To my mind, there are two hard and fast rules about this that I've taken from my experience dealing with separating parents. From the studies I've read and the real life situations I've witnessed over time, it's been pretty clear first of all that each kid will deal with the separation in his or her own way, and second of all that the best chance those kids will have in coping well with any separation anxieties they might have, is when they have two parents, or at least one parent, hell bent on putting their kids' needs first. So as for the second rule, you might not follow all the techniques or games I've mentioned here, but as I've said before, the very fact that you're reading about this suggests that you're one of those parents I'm talking about, that you're invested in the idea of putting your kids front and centre.

As for the first rule, put to one side all the neuroscience and psychology behind what's going on in your kids' minds right now. It's fairly cemented into reality that, in general, kids will be better off with two loving parents with whom they've formed a close attachment. Separation will tug at the strings of that attachment, and it's only by those two parents working together as much as possible to knot those strings back together despite the change of circumstances that will help minimise your kids' anxieties. And again, if that isn't possible given the acrimonious nature of your separation, or if your co-parent simply isn't interested, then don't let that stop you doing what you can, because your efforts in doing so of themselves will go a long way in helping you understand how *your* kids are getting on, and therefore, how you might communicate with and help them.

"delays in court procedure of one year represent only 2.5% of a 40 year old's life, but a whopping 25% of a four year old's. given the foundation of dispute that lies beneath them, legal proceedings lag behind kids' psychological needs as they develop..."

how can mediation help?

courting across the table

OK so first off you'll have picked up that I'm pretty biased in favour of mediation rather than dealing with family disputes through the courts. My feeling about that was borne from a long 14 years negotiating and arguing these types of disputes.

The reason I looked into accreditation in family mediation is that over time, I began to feel that in most of my family cases, it just didn't feel like the court was the most appropriate place to resolve the disputes I was dealing with. Particularly in cases involving children, although the court system tries its best, to my mind the outcome in cases has depended quite arbitrarily on which judge may be on the bench that day, and how well parties or their solicitors have managed to put across their views. In negotiations and decision making in family hearings, often I experienced a great deal of positional bargaining taking place which concerned the positions of each parent, but sometimes tended to put to one side the specific needs and development stages of the children. Again in my opinion, the impression I've had, not in all cases but certainly in a fair few, was that some negotiations and decisions were shaped by pre-suppositions, general attitudes and a 'let's meet halfway' approach, and although on occasions I was able to secure a 'result' which had been to the satisfaction of my clients, regularly I came away from the court with a sour feeling that the case could've been resolved more quickly and conclusively by getting the parties together for a properly constructed chat.

But that's just the way I feel. I know my opinion's not overly common around many family court practitioners in Scotland, and I'm certainly not advocating that if you're not doing mediation then you're not doing it right! So why bother with mediation? What's so special about it? And more to the point, what on earth has it to do with working out how to talk to your kids about separation?

getting legal advice

I can only talk from my experience as a solicitor in Scotland who's helped clients for years try and resolve their disputes arising from separation. I'm sure there are plenty of folks out there who are able to sort things out between themselves amicably and with minimum fuss. Those people may also benefit from some mediation, but at the very least I would say that it remains quite important that separating parents seek independent legal advice, even if they've worked things out without solicitors. The reason it's quite important is that you never know if things will turn sour down the line, say if one of you moves on to a new relationship, as it's at those times when verbal agreements tend to be flushed down the toilet. A solicitor can take what you've agreed, for example, and put it all into a binding agreement, and written documents like that are quite powerful should disputes arise in the future, or at the very least can provide separating parents with a foundation of trust to build on as time goes on - what you'd end up with in your hands would be a clear reflection that you and your co-parent have worked together to sort things out as amicably as you can for the sake of the kids. A solicitor can also advise you about the different methods you can use to resolve any conflict you have with your co-parent, and can refer you to mediation if that's the choice you decide to make.

the significance of delaying

I appreciate, of course, that getting to the stage of consensus that leads to a written agreement ain't always straightforward. Parents frustrated by how things are progressing will feel that if they place their interests in the hands of a judge, at the very least *something* will happen to progress things and, perhaps more enticingly, they'll think they might also get the teeth-crunching, mud-slinging royal rumble in court they've wanted with their co-parent since the separation.

In my experience though, in terms of moving things along that tends to be wishful thinking. I've seen some cases in court resolve pretty quickly. I've seen plenty more cases in court resolve quickly then rear their ugly head again when the settlement falls apart. I've seen even *more* cases in court that have gone on for months, years, and even in a couple of cases I've seen, the entire length of the kids' childhood.

Delays in legal procedure are pretty common. As I say, the court system does try its best and there are always reforms afoot that might make things a bit better. But that doesn't take away from the principle that if you take a family case to court, you're handing over control of the clock to someone else.

Here's something to think about. Delays in court procedure of one year represent only 2.5% of a 40 year old's life, but a whopping 25% of a four year old's. Given the foundation of dispute that lies beneath them, legal proceedings lag behind kids' psychological needs as they develop, so what's actually in their interests can change quite dramatically (and usually unnoticed) as the weeks and months roll on while it's being argued or negotiated in court, and it's in the nature of court proceedings in the real world that there's simply no time to explore properly the kids' needs from their own eyes. Yes, the court can order reports that might put across some more information to help the decision-making or negotiations about "contact" and "access", but the end result is pretty much always about just that, how much time each parent should have with the kids rather than what really needs to be done to address the kids' ever-changing development.

And the thing is, as time marches on kids can't be fully protected from the impact of court proceedings. It's been shown that attempts to conceal from the kids what's going on can lead to heightened anxiety and lack of trust, and for some kids a good percentage of their childhood is spent worrying about when the next court case will be. This is especially true around Christmas time which is a particularly busy period for the family courts. Year on year I witnessed the court timetable being crammed to the gunnels with cases where the parents were arguing over where their kids would wake up on Christmas morning, and on some occasions I noticed that it was the same parents coming back to court the next year for the same issue.

So even if you think you've been doing the right thing by dealing with your disputes in court, even telling your kids something as innocent as "mummy's going to court today to talk about you with daddy" will have an effect on them you might not realise. I'm no psychiatrist and

I'm not sure if you are either, but you might come to wonder what's going on in your kids' minds as time marches on and you're regularly talking about them with strange people. I've heard many parents talk about how their kids know words like "lawyer", "court", "contact visit", "daddy's rights", "mummy's contempt", and you might think like I do that this just seems pretty unnatural - that the kids have been exposed to words like this says more about their parents than it does about them, no matter whether each parent blames the other for teaching them words like that.

should court be avoided completely?

Now hey, I want to be clear that the court system is there for a reason. There are cases where dealing with the matter in court, even for part of the dispute, is entirely appropriate. And I've certainly no wish to suggest that the lawyers who deal with cases in court as I did for many a year are doing something wrong.

But, and it's a big but (no sniggering!), I've seen enough to know that arguing across the table with your co-parent isn't the best way to resolve your differences about the kids, and certainly not the best way to shield your kids from the impact of the separation. I can tell you, I've been involved in a number of cases involving kids where my client has actually *fist-pumped* the air when an order was granted in his or her favour. I mean really? Some of the behaviour and reactions like this I've experienced over the years have included such disturbing gems as "yeah, I've won!" and "did you see his face?!!". As you might imagine, when that kind of thing has happened, I've tended to leave the court with a pretty sour feeling that something just isn't right.

so what's mediation & how is it different?

Mediation is a process where you'll try to build agreement, to improve understanding, with the assistance of a trained mediator acting as an impartial third party. It's voluntary and aims to offer you the chance to be fully heard, to hear each other's perspectives and to decide for yourselves how to resolve your dispute.

The key principles of mediation are voluntariness, confidentiality, flexibility and impartiality.

The process empowers you and your co-parent to self-determine your own lives, and those of your kids, by unearthing any issues to be resolved, by exploring them from your own perspective and from your kids' eyes, by spending more time considering options rather than problems, by re-building trust, by helping you and your co-parent reform your relationship into a more parental one, and by crafting your own settlement. The mediator tries to keep the conversation constructive, forward-focussed, and at a pace you're both are comfortable with.

Using techniques like 'principled negotiation', mediation seeks to separate the people from the problem, to focus on interests rather than positions, to develop options for mutual gain, to focus on objectivity, and to consider the best alternatives to a negotiated agreement. The mediator acts completely impartially, is trained to recognise and manage power imbalance as it relates to, for example, emotions, intelligence, physicality, and the disclosure of information, and won't seek to arbitrate or pressure you into an agreement.

Mediation can explore in more detail with you how the separation has affected the kids. As I've said before, the separation may not be the only source of insecurity or unhappiness for young children, and the quality of the relationships they have with other adults, siblings, friends and even pets or toys can be way more significant. In other words, what matters more to your kids may differ greatly from just the amount of contact they have with each parent, and the things that matter to the kids will differ depending on their own stage of development. The way they're behaving towards you or your co-parent, or how they're getting on at school and so on, may be because of something completely opposite to what everyone might think.

So the depth and shifted focus of mediation can help you not only adjust yourselves, but can also help you work out how to guide and communicate with your kids as time goes on.

To give you an example, I know of one mediator who's placed an empty chair in the room, and asked the parties to speak to the chair about the separation as if their child was sitting on it. Sounds pretty weird I know, but it's just one of a myriad of techniques that has helped parents shift from their strongly-held positions to a state of mind that helps them understand what's really going on with their kids, what the kids' interests are no matter what their parents might think.

I can assure you, it might sound pretty wacky, but it can work. Sometimes it doesn't, but at the very least trying mediation might narrow some issues for negotiation and puts the control back firmly in your own hands, allowing you to take full responsibility for working out how to move on from the separation rather than leaving it to a judge or lawyers who might not know you or the kids from Adam.

so how does it all work?

First thing to do, therefore, is to ask your solicitor about all the ways of resolving your dispute. You'll hear a bit about negotiation, court, mediation, arbitration, collaborative law and things like that. My preference is mediation, but that's just me so it's best to explore all your options.

If, though, at some point before or after court proceedings have been raised you and your co-parent agree to be referred to mediation, both solicitors will contact a mediator.

If you have financial cover from the legal aid board, the mediator will ask the solicitors to seek enough funds to cover the cost of mediation. If only one of you has cover from the Board, usually the mediator will charge the other party at the same legal aid rate. If neither of you have cover with the legal aid board and are able to pay a mediator privately, you can actually agree between yourselves which mediator to contact and approach him or her directly (if like me you're in Scotland, please have a look at the CALM Scotland site in the resources section later to search for mediators local to you).

The mediator will ask your solicitor for your contact details (or you if you've approached the mediator directly), and will not need anything other than your ID. You'll be sent terms and conditions, a referral form and some information about the mediation process, and will then arrange with the mediator a first session. My approach is usually to arrange individual sessions in the first instance, basically to help ease you into the process and learn a little about its different methods before you head into a joint session.

At the first individual session the mediator will explain the mediation process, gather from you some information and note any issues you'd like to be addressed. The mediator generally will also assess the suitability for joint mediation sessions as well as screen for domestic abuse or any other issues that might suggest that mediation is inappropriate. As well as that, there will be an assessment as to whether co-mediating with another mediator might be a good idea, for example where at least one of you isn't really forthcoming or talkative and another body in the room might help keep the conversation flowing. If there is to be a co-mediation, consideration will be given as to whether the other mediator should be male or female depending on the circumstances, so this should all be explained to you.

If after each individual session mediation is to proceed, a joint session will be arranged at a convenient time for all concerned. At that session you will each be given plenty of opportunity to identify your concerns and so on, and after that will discuss with the mediator how best to address those concerns, setting an agenda for a constructive dialogue.

Further sessions will likely be arranged, either joint or separate depending on the circumstances, until the mediation reaches a conclusion.

At any point during or at the end of the process you can ask the mediator to prepare an interim or final mediation summary of what has been discussed. That summary would not be admissible as evidence in court, but could be released to the solicitors if you both wish. The summary would identify the main issues explored at mediation and also any consensus reached, so it might assist, for example, in the preparation of a written agreement I was talking about before. Alternatively you can work together with your mediator to outline the terms of a parenting plan that will set out not only the future living arrangements being put in place, but also the ground rules and mechanisms or techniques you've both agreed to apply for things relating to education, health, discipline, the introduction of future partners, and so on.

Once mediation is at an end the mediator would submit the account for payment, but generally you would be free to be referred back for future sessions if you wished.

So like I say, there are other options available and it's important that you're comfortable with how you think your issues should be addressed. You can find more information about all this in the resources section. Of course, I should also reiterate that what I've just yapped on about concerns mediation in Scotland, so if you're reading this and live elsewhere, again make sure you ask your lawyer or otherwise approach a mediation service first to learn a bit more. Bear in mind though that wherever you live, the principles like self-determination and impartiality that define mediation are the same the world over – why else do you think businesses and even governments are using it more frequently as well these days?!!

the glass cube

To finish up this section I'd like to leave you with some food for thought, a little imagery for you to consider before you start or continue any discussions, negotiations, arguments with your ex about your kids' best interests.

As an aside, I'll throw my hands up and admit that it really gets on my wick when I hear parents or lawyers talk about 'best interests'. *It's in my kids' best interests that...* – another label for you that's misused each and every day and is notoriously difficult to break down. But given that it's a common term, here's what I think:
I'm going to give you two statements about you and your ex, and I want you to think about both of them very carefully.

1. Each of you has different ideas about what's in the best interests of your kids.
2. Each of you thinks you're right.

Now be truthful. Do you think those two statements are pretty accurate?

88

If you do, then what you've done there is to adopt a position. Between you and your ex, you've built for yourselves in your minds a clear, glass cube. Any argument you have about your kids' best interests, therefore, will be based around those positions, confined within this glass cube you've both constructed. And by virtue of that confinement, any possible outcome from that argument won't be able to escape the glass cube, because you've both chosen freely to define the boundaries of your argument.

The thing about being in a glass cube, however, is that over time the oxygen starts to run out. So without breathing space, you'll find that the argument gets stale and begins to repeat itself, bouncing endlessly as it does off the walls of the cube. As a result, you end up getting nowhere, and all the dreams each of you might have had for your kids, all those best interests you're kicking about tiresomely inside the cube, begin to choke and die.

I don't know your kids. I'm willing to bet, though, that they'll see right through the walls of your glass cube. Remember that they'll see themselves as half of you and half of your ex. So when they peer in and see their parents argue, when they see you not being civil to each other at handover, when they don't hear you talk positively about their other parent, as they get older they might come to think that, actually, you've *enjoyed* your time in the glass cube, that you've been faced with a free choice as responsible parents and have decided to argue about your kids' best interests rather than thinking, instead, *well maybe it's in their best interests for us just to try and get along for their sake*.

So before you immerse yourself in the minutiae, the nitty gritty of that next argument with your ex; before you yelp and scowl about your parental rights, or when the kids should be with you, or why your ex is wrong about this or about that, or why if you don't get what you want you'll go to court, or why your hands are tied because your ex ain't budging from that ignorant position, however justified you might feel in pursuing that line; just pause for a minute there, take a deep breath, think about the big picture and answer as truthfully as you can this one little question:

Given the choice, do you really, genuinely want to hold onto your kids' "best interests" forever within this glass cube you've built, starved of oxygen, or do you want to smash it to pieces and let them breathe again?

I know there are important things to work out, and I'm not advocating that you just throw up the white flag for the sake of peace. I also appreciate that despite your wishes, your ex might leave you little choice, particularly where there's been some domestic abuse and the like. What I'm saying here is that if you'd like to get out of that glass cube, if you'd like to deal with any issues about your kids in a responsible, constructive manner, if you want to build a working parental relationship for the future that closes off the one you had previously with your ex, if you want to move on and enjoy the rest of your lives rather than leaving your kids suffocated and defined by the separation (...*phew*, that's a lot of "if's"...)

...then the choice to do so is sitting firmly in the hands of both of you.

"The simple process of sitting down before bed with your kids to read to them encourages a bond that you might not fully appreciate but which your kids will feel deep down. Reading books designed for kids in these circumstances can help them start to acknowledge and understand the types of feelings they've been experiencing after the separation, and to appreciate that those feelings are perfectly normal."

resources

introduction

I've placed this resources section before the conclusion as I think it's pretty important and I always get the impression that this type of section can be skipped very easily if it's been left to the tail-end of a book. Think of it as like the bottom of a mug of instant hot chocolate – if you take some of the chocolate powder that's settled down at the bottom of the mug and mix it up again with the rest, *boy* does the drink get more tasty!

books for your kids to read

Reading with your kids is always recommended no matter whether you've gone through a separation, but as you might imagine, it becomes even more vital if you have. The simple process of sitting down before bed with your kids to read to them encourages a bond that you might not fully appreciate but which your kids will feel deep down. Reading books designed for kids in these circumstances can help them start to acknowledge and understand the types of feelings they've been experiencing after the separation, and to appreciate that those feelings are perfectly normal.

As they get older, of course, they'll prefer reading themselves, so browse around for these and any other books you think might be helpful for your kids to read with you or alone, and if they do want to read alone, encourage them gently to do so.

So here are just a few that I've come across and which I know have helped parents and their kids in the past:

Two Homes by Claire Mansurel – for 3-5 years olds
It's Not Your Fault, Koko Bear by Vicki Lansky & Jane Prince – for 3-7 year olds
The Huge Bag of Worries by Virginia Ironside – for 4-8 year olds
Dinosaurs Divorce by Laurene Krasny Brown & Marc Brown – for 6-8 year olds
The Suitcase Kid by Jacqueline Wilson – for 6-12 year olds
What In the World Do You Do When Your Parents Divorce by Kent Winchester – for 8-10 year olds
Goggle Eyes by Anne Fine – for 8-12 year olds

books & materials for you to read

What do you mean *I've read this book so don't need anything else?!!*

There are plenty of books and materials dotted around that can help your communication with your kids, as well as on the other things you have to think about following your separation. As I've said before, when it comes to the legal or financial side of things, you're best advised to seek advice from a lawyer and financial or money adviser rather than trying to work it out from reading materials you've picked up, so the resources here are more focused on the emotional and planning aspects that tend to arise.

The Complete Guide to Divorced Parenting by Christopher Mills
Talking to Children About Divorce – Positive Conversations by Sue Atkins
The Guide for Separated Parents: Putting Children First by Karen & Nick Woodall
Help Your Children Cope With Your Divorce by Paula Hall (Relate)
Adult Children of Parental Alienation Syndrome by Amy J. L. Baker
The Truth About Children And Divorce by Robert Emery
Love Lose Live (fictional novel) by Mary Banham-Hall

websites for your kids to browse

Letting your kids loose online might sound to the older generations like total madness! These days though, kids are growing up immersed in all things technological and internet-based. It's just the way it is, and provided they understand from you the proper safeguards about spending time online, they'll learn a whole lot from websites. Some of it will be good, some of it complete nonsense, some of it just plain wrong, but the exploration and information-gathering is something that to my mind needs to be encouraged rather than feared. Again, if you've spent enough energy on maintaining a positive relationship with your kids, maintaining that open conversation after the separation, you might find that they'll pick up things online about separation and test with you the veracity of what they've learned.

The important point here as we think about how you'll be talking to your kids about separation, is that pointing out books and sites to your kids and letting them explore for themselves, is another means of telling them that you want to help them through all this.

To be frank, most of the websites about separation online are geared more for parents than for kids, and maybe that's because it's simply assumed these days that as kids learn to browse the internet they'll be able to access every site anyway so shouldn't be patronised by being directed towards dumbed-down guides, but here are a few you might want to look at.

childline.org.uk

Childline is a free 24 hour private and confidential counselling service for kids up to their 19th birthday. It's run by the National Society for the Prevention of Cruelty to Children (NSPCC), which although is a charity based outside Scotland, runs the service throughout the UK. From the website your kids can find the telephone numbers, online chat details and email addresses for contacting Childline. They can also browse the site and learn a great deal about what issues they might be going through in simpler, plain English language that's easier for them to understand.

thesite.org

This is a site designed for 16-25 year olds. It's run by YouthNet and provides non-judgemental support and information on everything from sex and exam stress to debt and drugs. Again it's a 24 hour service with online chat and a well-populated forum, with articles and real-life experiences retold around the site.

voicesinthemiddle.org

This is a site run by Kids the Middle, a campaign designed to ensure the UN Convention on the Rights of the Children is adhered to, meaning essentially that kids are listened to when decisions are being taken that concern them. The site is built and operated by young people to meet the information needs of kids in separating families, and is gaining a great deal of traction as this book goes to print.

familybreakups.com

Another one that opened more recently in England is Family Breakups, a collaboration of Oxfordshire Family Mediation, Oxfordshire Youth Arts Project, and four local schools. It's full of tips, stories, advice, support, music / film / book / activity suggestions, all based on what's actually helped kids deal with family breakups. It gives answers to burning questions on breakups and gives you advice and coping mechanisms to consider, once again confirming that your kids don't have to feel alone in what they're going through after the separation.

websites for you to browse

calmscotland.co.uk

CALM stands for comprehensive accredited lawyer mediators. Phew! It's the collection of trained mediators in Scotland that I'm part of, and you can browse the site to find out more about how mediation can help you talk through the issues arising from your separation. As I've said earlier, mediation can help you not only sort these things out, but can also guide you both through how to talk to your kids about the separation. The website provides you with all the details you need to get this process started, but please let me know if you want any more information.

relationships-scotland.org.uk

Relationships Scotland is another mediation provider, and also helps individuals, couples and families with counselling, child contact centres and other family support services around the country. For many years they've been a national voice for relationship services and influence political and legislative policy development in the family support area, but more importantly for you it's best to take a look around the site and see how they can help you in your time of need.

children1st.org.uk

This charity is geared towards ensuring every child and young person in Scotland has a happy, health, safe and secure childhood. Its relevance to you in the separation is that it has a whack of information on the site to help you guide your kids during this difficult time in your life, and that it also directs you towards its advice lines for single parents. It's a really valuable resource and I recommend that if you haven't done already you should take a look and see how it might help you.

partnershipforchildren.org.uk

This is an English charity but is concerned with the mental health and well-being of children around the world. There is a whopping amount of supportive information for parents trying to guide their kids through separation. Just type in "separation" into their search box and it'll open up for you a great deal to read and think about, particularly on the subject of kids' anxieties.

kidshealth.org

I really like this site, as it could quite as easily have been listed as a site for kids to visit as well as adults. It's one of the world's most popular sites about parenting issues and, well, kids' health (who'd have thunk it?!!), and is designed so that it can be accessed from the eyes of a younger child, teen or adult. Again use the search box to hone into the advice about separation.

parentingacrossscotland.org

This is a partnership of a number of like-minded charities and is funded by the Scottish Government. In the site there's a wealth of information for families and family practitioners, but for me the publication section of essays, tips and other materials is extremely valuable for those looking for some guidance on parenting in, well, Scotland!

helguide.org

This is an outstanding resource for many personal and emotional issues you might experience in life, and if you had the time you could spend endless hours meandering through its self-help pages and picking up innovative, inspirational advice for how to move past those issues. In relation to separation, type that into the search box on the site and you'll open up a mineshaft of guidance to point you in the right direction.

sueatkinsparentingcoach.com

Sue Atkins is an internationally renowned parenting expert, speaker, author and broadcaster you may have seen on TV, including on ITV's This Morning, or heard on radio. In her wonderful website there is a wealth of information, courses and resources directed at the various challenges you can face as a parent, including in separation.

thejaneevans.com

Jane has taken her personal relationship experience in the past and, following time spent in early years care & education and then as a foster carer, moved onto become a well known expert in parenting and family support. She has appeared on TV and radio for her work, and her inspirational TED talk on her 'meerkat' brain model has been accessed by thousands across the world. Her main area of coaching can help you consider more carefully the anxiety arising from separation, in children and in yourself.

one final practical tool for joint parenting

I'm a bit of a tech geek as well as an armchair psychologist. One of things I've found getting in the way of communication with kids in a separation is all the confused chat about "the schedule". Like, who's getting the kids on such and such date? In my experience, much of this chat is uttered in front of the kids.

Now in the days of old before they invented fire, the wheel, and so on, separated parents might have used a diary to organise their kids' time. Per Luke Dunphy on the superb tv show, Modern Family:

"Wake up and smell the internet, Grandma!"

Get a secure shared drive online. This could be, for example, Google Drive or OneDrive. Upload onto the drive a calendar, and fill it with the living arrangements schedule, birthdays, dates and times of upcoming parties, school parents' evenings and events, medical appointments. That said, a drive like this could do *so* much more than this. Upload key contact lists, photos, videos, your kids' Christmas or birthday present lists marked with who's to get what, a breakdown of any kids' expenses to be reimbursed, school reports and notes about health or education issues arising, reasons why your kid's been grounded, a virtual 'school bag' of what they'll need at school in the coming week, a list of your kids' current favourite books or interests or music or tv shows or...well, you get the picture.

Share that drive with your co-parent so that you can both update everything on it. No longer any need to get confused in front of your kids about such stuff, therefore, again minimising any anxieties they might have about their lives with separated parents. This way it can be accessed and updated by both of you wherever you are from a PC, laptop, tablet, smartphone, smartwatch, and no doubt in the coming few years, from your family robot! And it's all free.

And no, I'm not being sponsored by Google or Microsoft!...

that bottom line again

How many times have I mentioned *the bottom line* in this book?!!

So anywho, as you might imagine, the resources I've included here represent only the tip of the iceberg when it comes to information and guidance online. Much of that information is for free, so even if you don't visit or pick up the ones I've listed here, make sure you take from this the message that learning from others about what you might be going through can be extremely helpful, and as such, you should never think that you're on your own in all this.

"more than anything else, when all is said and done, the most powerful influence on a child comes in the form of watching the parents' behaviour."

conclusion

the pencilled outline

So there we go. I guarantee that having read this little book, you'll have no more issues or concerns about talking with your kids about your separation.

(legal note – guarantees will not be honoured) ☺

As I mentioned at the outset, this is just a little nudge in the right direction. Much of what you've read here might have come across as pretty generic. My excuse for that is that without seeing you face to face, it's difficult to know exactly what your situation entails. What I've tried to do is to lay out some broad ideas and principles based on the many parents I've spoken to or represented over the years, so that hopefully, you're left with a pencilled outline you can colour in with your own crayons and pens.

I appreciate 100% that it's hard right now for you to focus so much on how to talk to your kids whilst at the same time trying to work out how you're going to get through your own issues, your own new life that's beginning to spiral round you like a whirlwind. Like I said before, don't beat yourself up – you've shown by reading this that you're invested in the idea that your kids will need you more than ever, and if you continue to take those deep breaths and pace yourself, if you dip in and out of this and any other books or resources you can find, if you lean on all the friends and family and professionals happy to lend you an ear, and most importantly if you look after your own health and wellbeing, you may well come to realise that there's a great life to be had after your separation and all it takes to get there is for you to focus every day on your relationship with your kids.

Take one step at a time each conversation you have with them, listen to them, and as time goes on I know you'll get there.

parents as gods

I wanted to finish off by quoting Gary Direnfeld again, as I think it ties things up quite nicely and leaves you with an important message to think about. It's from his excellent book *Raising Kids Without Raising Cane*. Here it is:

As parents, we are as gods in our children's lives. Children come into this world totally helpless, dependent on us for survival. The newborn has basic reflexes and many needs. With proper care and nurturing, the child develops. Throughout, the child must be fed, sheltered, clothed, cleaned and loved. Without at least one caring adult, the child will surely die.

Toddlers, preschoolers and young school-age children continue to be dependent on grown-ups, particularly their parents, for food, shelter, clothing, love, guidance and protection.

Because of our position in our children's lives, we are of the utmost importance to them. Children will seek to please their gods, as best they can, no matter what. Children will use their gods as models of behaviour and will copy the behaviour they observe.

More than anything else, when all is said and done, the most powerful influence on a child comes in the form of watching the parents' behaviour.

feedback

It's very important to me that you get the most out of this little book. I'd love to hear how you get on with it in the real world, so please make sure you leave a comment on Amazon or follow and chat with me on twitter @thecalmmediator. If you've found it helpful in your situation, leaving comments can be really handy in spreading the word, as I certainly look at reviews before I think about getting a book, so many thanks in advance if you're comfortable doing so.

Also, if you are in the Glasgow area and wish to go ahead with family mediation with me, please just suggest this to your solicitor who will make the necessary arrangements, or come to me directly in the event that you're not assisted via the legal aid board.

Thank you so much for picking up a copy of this book, and I really hope that it helps you maintain a loving and healthy connection with your kids as time goes on after the separation. I wish you the very best of luck in resolving any issues you may have.

Cheers,

Scott

separate | mediate | move on
accredited by the law society of scotland in family mediation
www.twitter.com/thecalmmediator

legal stuff

means, electronic, mechanical, photocopying, recording or otherwise, without the prior permission in writing of Scott Charles Docherty.

ISBN-13: 978-1512212495
ISBN-10: 1512212490

With thanks to the Centre for Health Equality Studies (CHESS), Stockholm University / Karolinska Institutet, the Joseph Rowntree Foundation, Resolution, and Gary Direnfeld for reference to their respective research publications or work referenced throughout this book.

relying on the book

This book is not intended to be a substitute for legal and other advice relating to separation. The reader should regularly consult with a solicitor, mediator, counsellor and other professional individuals and organisations to ensure his or her interests and those of his or her child or children are safeguarded and promoted. The author advises that the reader takes full responsibility for his or her actions in handling all matters arising from his or her separation.

This book is designed to provide information only on talking to children about separation. This information is provided and sold with the knowledge that the author does not offer any legal or other professional advice. In the case of a need for any such advice, again it is advisable to consult with an appropriate professional. This book does not contain all information available on the subject. This book has not been created to be specific to any individual's or organisation's situation or needs. Every effort has been made to make this book as accurate as possible. However, there may be typographical and / or content errors. Therefore, this book should serve only as a general guide and not as the ultimate source of subject information. This book contains information that might be dated and is intended only to educate and entertain. The author shall have no liability or responsibility to any person or entity regarding any loss or damage incurred, or alleged to have incurred, directly or indirectly, by the information contained in this book. The reader agrees to be bound by this disclaimer or otherwise may return this book in terms of the relevant statutory and commercial provisions applicable.

Any links to websites listed in this book are provided for informational purposes only, and do not constitute endorsement of any products or services provided by these websites. The links are also subject to change, may expire, or be redirected without any notice.

Equally, any reference to reference materials in this book are provided for informational purposes only, and the author accepts no responsibility for any loss, damages or consequences arising from the reader's use of such materials. It is the reader's sole responsibility to check the accuracy or provenance of such materials.

and please keep an eye out on amazon for this...

how to talk to your ex after
separation

by scott c docherty

Printed in Great
Britain
by Amazon

32437664R00071